I0893125

DETROIT LIONS

BY JOSH ANDERSON

Stride
An Imprint of The Child's World®
childsworld.com

The Child's World
childsworld.com

Published by The Child's World®
800-599-READ • www.childsworld.com

Copyright © 2023 by The Child's World®
All rights reserved. No part of this book may be reproduced or utilized in any form of by any means without written permission from the publisher.

Photography Credits
Cover: Rey Del Rio / Stringer / Getty Images; page 1: © Africa Studio / Shutterstock; page 3: © Ronald Martinez / Staff / Getty Images; page 5: © Quinn Harris / Stringer / Getty Images; page 6: © Jonathan Daniel / Stringer / Getty Images; page 9: © Steve Dykes / Stringer / Getty Images; page 10: © Gregory Shamus / Stringer / Getty Images; page 11: © stevezmina1 / Getty Images; page 12: © Rey Del Rio / Stringer / Getty Images; page 12: © Mitchell Leff / Stringer / Getty Images; page 13: © Leon Halip / Stringer / Getty Images; page 13: © Jim McIsaac / Staff / Getty Images; page 14: © Leon Halip / Stringer / Getty Images; page 15: © Tom Pidgeon / Stringer / Getty Images; page 16: © Leon Halip / Stringer / Getty Images; page 16: © Jay Publishing / Wikimedia; page 17: © Jonathan Daniel / Stringer / Getty Images; page 17: © Jay Publishing / Wikimedia; page 18: © Hall of Fame / Associated Press; page 18: © AP / Associated Press; page 19: © Jonathan Daniel / Staff / Getty Images; page 19: © Gregory Shamus / Staff / Getty Images; page 20: © Gregory Shamus / Staff / Getty Images; page 20: © Wesley Hitt / Stringer / Getty Images; page 21: © Gregory Shamus / Staff / Getty Images; page 21: © Gregory Shamus / Staff / Getty Images; page 22: © Rick Stewart / Stringer / Getty Images; page 23: © Matthew Stockman / Staff / Getty Images; page 23: © stevezmina1 / Getty Images; page 25: © Rick Stewart / Stringer / Getty Images; page 26: © Doug Pensinger / Staff / Getty Images; page 29: © Ronald Martinez / Staff / Getty Images

ISBN Information
9781503857858 (Reinforced Library Binding)
9781503860483 (Portable Document Format)
9781503861848 (Online Multi-user eBook)
9781503863200 (Electronic Publication)

LCCN 2021952700

Printed in the United States of America

BRINGING THE WORLD TO YOUNG READERS 1968

TABLE OF CONTENTS

GO LIONS!

The Detroit Lions compete in the National Football **League's** (NFL's) National Football Conference (NFC). They play in the NFC North **division**, along with the Chicago Bears, Green Bay Packers, and Minnesota Vikings. Detroit is home to one of the NFL's oldest traditions. In 1934, the team's owner decided he wanted to host a game on Thanksgiving Day. Since then, the Lions have hosted a Thanksgiving game every season. Let's learn more about the Lions!

NFC NORTH DIVISION

Chicago Bears

Detroit Lions

Green Bay Packers

Minnesota Vikings

JARED GOFF (LEFT) TOOK OVER AS THE LIONS' QUARTERBACK IN 2021.

BECOMING THE LIONS

The team was formed in 1928 and was originally called the Portsmouth Spartans. They played in Portsmouth, Ohio, until 1934, when their owner moved them to Detroit, Michigan. The team's name was changed to Lions after the move. They won their first ten games after moving to their new home. The Lions won four NFL Championships in the era before the **Super Bowl**. They haven't gotten to play in a Super Bowl yet, but fans hope that will change sometime soon.

BILLY SIMS RUSHED FOR MORE THAN 5,000 YARDS IN FIVE SEASONS WITH THE LIONS.

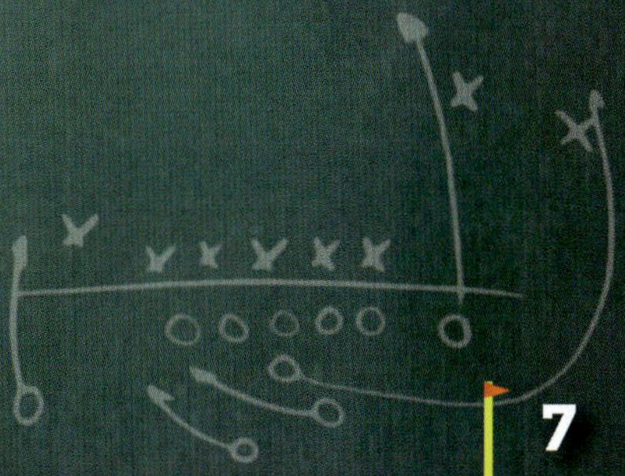

BY THE NUMBERS

FOUR
NFL Championships for the Lions in the Pre–Super Bowl era

12
wins for the Lions in 1991

474
points scored by the team in 2011—a Lions' record!

6,113
total yards gained in 1995—most in the NFL!

THE LIONS EARNED A TRIP TO THE PLAYOFFS IN 2016 AND FACED THE SEATTLE SEAHAWKS.

FORD FIELD HAS ALSO HOSTED THE NCAA MEN'S BASKETBALL TOURNAMENT AND WRESTLEMANIA.

GAME DAY

Since 2002, the Lions have played their home games at Ford Field. For more than three decades, the team shared Tiger **Stadium** with the city's Major League Baseball team, the Detroit Tigers. Ford Field is a domed stadium, which means the building has a curved roof. The stadium honors Detroit's rich history. Ford Field's frosted glass roof is meant to look like the design of many of the car factories in Detroit. And one whole side of the stadium is connected to a 1920s Hudson's Department Store warehouse. Ford Field holds 65,000 Lions fans on game days.

We're Famous!

In 1963, an author with no football experience convinced the Lions to allow him to participate in their preseason training camp. George Plimpton wrote a famous book called *Paper Lion* about trying to make the team. He'd hoped to get to actually play in a preseason game, but the NFL wouldn't allow it.

UNIFORM

BLUE

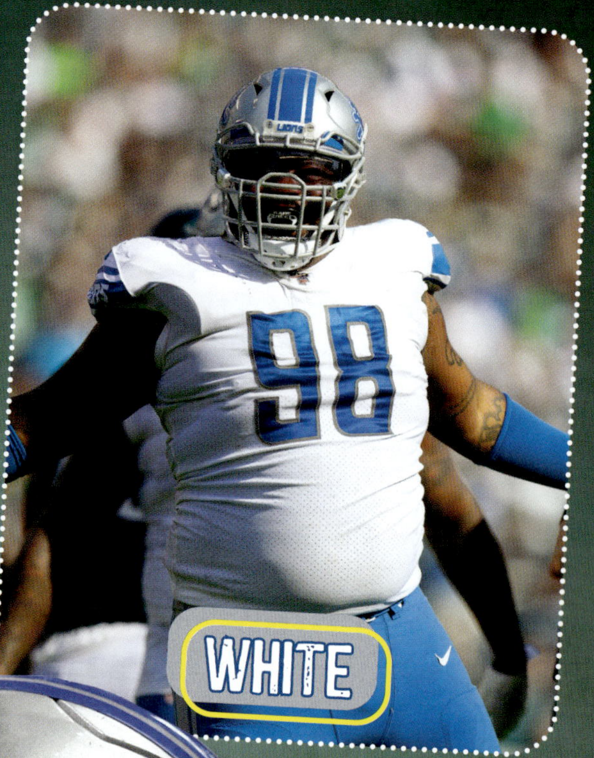

WHITE

Truly Weird

Hall of Fame wide receiver Calvin Johnson had a game for the ages in 2013. In the Lions 31–30 win over the Cowboys, Johnson caught 14 passes and gained 329 yards receiving. That's the second-most receiving yards ever gained in a single game. Johnson actually had more yards himself than the entire Cowboys team combined!

Alternate Jersey

Sometimes teams wear an alternate jersey that is different from their home and away jerseys. It might be a bright color or have a unique theme. To celebrate the Lions' 75th anniversary, the team wore "throwback" uniforms for a game in 2008 against the Jacksonville Jaguars.The look turned out to be unlucky for the Lions. They lost the game 38–14.

LIONS PLAYERS ENTER FORD FIELD THROUGH A GIANT CLOUD OF SMOKE ON GAME DAYS.

TEAM SPIRIT

Going to a game at Ford Field can be tons of fun! The team's fight song is called "Gridiron Heroes," and it's sung each time the Lions score a **touchdown** at home. The Lions Cheerleaders entertain the crowd during breaks in the action and at halftime. Joining the cheer squad is Roary the Lion. He's the team's mascot. Roary is a costumed lion who wears the team's jersey. Fans who come to the game hungry might enjoy smoked buffalo chicken tatchos. Tatchos are a delicious combination of tater tots and nachos!

ROARY

HEROES OF HISTORY

Calvin Johnson

Wide Receiver | 2007–2015

Nicknamed "Megatron," Johnson set the single-season record when he gained 1,964 receiving yards in 2012. He had more than 1,000 yards in seven of nine seasons. Johnson played in six **Pro Bowls**. His 122 catches in 2012 are the tenth most ever in a single season. He's a member of the Pro Football Hall of Fame.

Bobby Layne

Quarterback | 1950–1958

Layne led the Lions to three NFL Championships during his time with the team. Known for being his best when the game was on the line, it was his last-second pass that won the 1953 Championship. Layne led the league in passing yards twice. He was inducted into the Pro Football Hall of Fame in 1967.

Herman Moore

Wide Receiver | 1991–2001

Moore led the Lions in receiving for six-straight seasons. His 123 catches in 1995 are the ninth most ever in a single season. He totaled more than 1,000 yards four times and had 62 receiving touchdowns in his career. Moore was chosen for the Pro Bowl four times.

Joe Schmidt

Linebacker | 1953–1965

Schmidt was a key part of two Lions teams that won the NFL Championship. He had 24 interceptions in his career. Schmidt's eight fumble recoveries in 1955 is one short of the record for a defensive player. He's a member of the Pro Football Hall of Fame.

The Lions win their first NFL Championship over the New York Giants.

The Lions come back from 20 points down in the Western Conference Championship game and defeat the San Francisco 49ers 31–27.

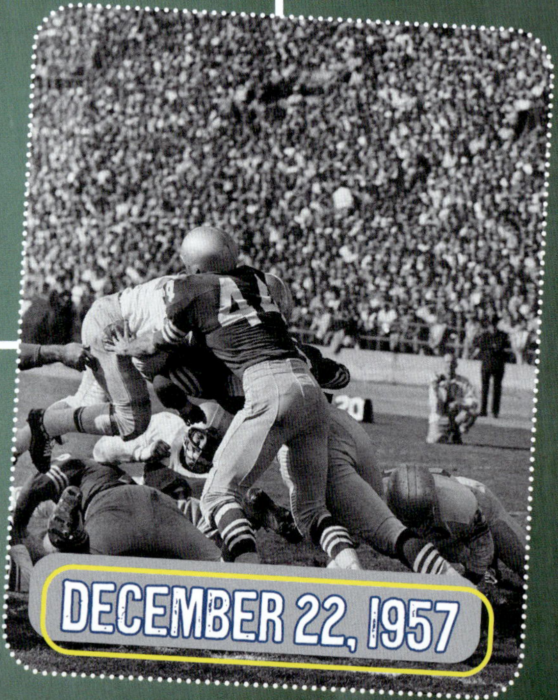

BIG DAYS

DECEMBER 30, 2012

Calvin Johnson sets the single-season record for receiving yards in a game against the Chicago Bears.

APRIL 29, 2021

The Lions select Penei Sewell, an offensive tackle from the University of Oregon, with the seventh pick in the NFL Draft.

MODERN-DAY MARVELS

Jared Goff

Quarterback | Debut: 2021

Goff was originally picked by the Los Angeles Rams with the first overall pick in the NFL Draft. After leading the Rams to one Super Bowl and three trips to the **playoffs**, Goff was traded to the Lions in 2021. Goff has been chosen for the Pro Bowl twice in his career.

T. J. Hockenson

Tight End | Debut: 2019

In 2020, "Hock" became the first Lions tight end to make it to the Pro Bowl in more than 20 years. During his first three seasons combined, Hockenson totaled more than 1,500 yards receiving and caught 12 touchdowns. His 131 yards in his first game set an NFL record for tight ends.

Frank Ragnow

Center | Debut: 2018

After starring at the University of Arkansas, Ragnow was the Lions' first-round draft pick in 2018. He has started every game he's played for the team during his career. In 2020, he became the first Lions center in two decades to be chosen for the Pro Bowl.

D'Andre Swift

Running Back | Debut: 2020

Swift is a running back who's equally as dangerous running the ball or catching a pass. He was the Lions' second round pick in the 2020 NFL Draft. Swift totaled 878 yards as a rookie in 2020 and scored ten touchdowns. In 2021, Swift had 1,069 total yards and seven touchdowns for the Lions.

SANDERS WAS CHOSEN FOR THE NFL'S 100TH ANNIVERSARY ALL-TIME TEAM.

THE GOAT

GREATEST OF ALL TIME

BARRY SANDERS

Sanders never totaled fewer than 1,115 rushing yards in a season. He's the fourth-leading rusher in NFL history. Sanders led the league in rushing four times. Considered by some to be the best running back in league history, Sanders won the 1997 **Most Valuable Player** (MVP) Award. He helped lead the Lions to the playoffs five times. Sanders is a member of the Pro Football Hall of Fame.

FAN FAVORITE

Jason Hanson–Kicker

1992–2012

No one has spent more consecutive seasons with the same team than Hanson did with the Lions. He's beloved by fans for his 21-straight seasons in silver and blue. During that time, Hanson scored 2,150 points. That's the fourth most in NFL history!

THE BIG GAME

JANUARY 5, 1992 – DIVISIONAL PLAYOFF ROUND

Coming into their divisional round game against the Dallas Cowboys, the Lions hadn't won a postseason game since 1957. The powerful Cowboys team included several future Hall of Famers. The Lions jumped out to an early lead when quarterback Erik Kramer tossed a 31-yard touchdown to Willie Green. They built on their lead from there. By the time franchise legend Barry Sanders ran for a 47-yard touchdown in the fourth quarter, the game was already decided. The Lions' 38–6 playoff win was their first in more than three decades.

ERIK KRAMER COMPLETED 29 PASSES FOR 341 AND 3 TOUCHDOWNS IN THE LIONS' DIVISIONAL PLAYOFF VICTORY OVER THE DALLAS COWBOYS.

WAYNE FONTES LED THE TEAM TO 66 VICTORIES BETWEEN 1988 AND 1996.

AMAZING FEATS

5,038 Passing Yards

In 2011 by
QUARTERBACK
Matthew Stafford

16 Receiving Touchdowns

In 2011 by
WIDE RECEIVER
Calvin Johnson

15 Sacks

In 1999 by
DEFENSIVE END
Robert Porcher

12 Interceptions

In 1953 by
SAFETY
Jack Christiansen

ALL-TIME BEST

PASSING YARDS

Matthew Stafford
45,109

Bobby Layne
15,710

Scott Mitchell
12,647

RUSHING YARDS

Barry Sanders
15,269

Billy Sims
5,106

Dexter Bussey
5,105

RECEIVING YARDS

Calvin Johnson
11,619

Herman Moore
9,174

Johnnie Morton
6,499

SACKS*

Alex Karras
100

Robert Porcher
95.5

Al Baker
74

SCORING

Jason Hanson
2,150

Eddie Murray
1,113

Matt Prater
768

INTERCEPTIONS

Dick LeBeau
62

Lem Barney
56

Yale Lary
50

*unofficial before 1982

THE LIONS CHOSE MATTHEW STAFFORD FIRST OVERALL IN THE 2009 NFL DRAFT.

GLOSSARY

division (dih-VIZSH-un): a group of teams within the NFL who play each other more frequently and compete for the best record

Hall of Fame (HAHL of FAYM): a museum in Canton, Ohio, that honors the best players in NFL history

league (LEEG): an organization of sports teams that compete against each other

Most Valuable Player (MOHST VAHL-yuh-bul PLAY-uhr): a yearly award given to the top player in the NFL

playoffs (PLAY-ahfs): a series of games played after the regular season that decides which two teams play in the Super Bowl

Pro Bowl (PRO BOWL): the NFL's All-Star game where the best players in the league compete

sack (SAK): when a quarterback is tackled behind the line of scrimmage before he can throw the ball

stadium (STAY-dee-uhm): a building with a field and seats for fans where teams play

Super Bowl (SOO-puhr BOWL): the championship game of the NFL, played between the winners of the AFC and the NFC

touchdown (TUTCH-down): a play in which the ball is brought into the other team's end zone, resulting in six points

FIND OUT MORE

IN THE LIBRARY

Bulgar, Beth and Mark Bechtel. *My First Book of Football.* New York, NY: Time Inc. Books, 2015.

Jacobs, Greg. *The Everything Kids' Football Book, 7th Edition*. Avon, MA: Adams Media, 2021.

Peterson, Justin. *Detroit Lions*. New York, NY: AV2, 2020.

Sports Illustrated Kids. *The Greatest Football Teams of All Time*. New York, NY: Time Inc. Books, 2018.

ON THE WEB

Visit our website for links about the Detroit Lions:
childsworld.com/links

Note to parents, teachers, and librarians: We routinely verify our web links to make sure they are safe and active sites. Encourage your readers to check them out!

INDEX

ABOUT THE AUTHOR

Josh Anderson has published over 50 books for children and young adults. His two boys are the greatest joys in his life. Hobbies include coaching his sons in youth basketball, no-holds-barred games of Apples to Apples, and taking long family walks. His favorite NFL team is a secret he'll never share!